A Guide to
THE SAINSBURY WING
at the National Gallery

MICHAEL WILSON

D1305203

NATIONAL GALLERY PUBLICATIONS, LONDON

First published in Great Britain in 1991 by
National Gallery Publications Limited
5/6 Pall Mall East, London SW1Y 5BA

British Library Cataloguing in Publication Data
Wilson, Michael, *1951 Aug. 13–*
    A Guide to the Sainsbury Wing at the National Gallery.
    1. National Gallery. Great Britain 2. Paintings 3. Europe
    I. Title
    759.94074

    ISBN 0-947645-94-2

Designed by Simon Bell
Printed in Great Britain by
William Clowes Limited, Beccles and London

ABOVE
The Agony in the Garden, *c.* 1460, by
Andrea Mantegna.

TITLE PAGE
Portrait of a Lady in Yellow, *c.* 1465,
by Alesso Baldovinetti.

FRONT COVER
The diminishing perspective to the left
of the grand staircase, looking
towards Cima's great altarpiece, *The
Incredulity of Saint Thomas*, *c.* 1504.

BACK COVER
The Rape of Helen, *c.* 1450, by a
follower of Fra Angelico.

Contents

Foreword

THIS IS A SMALL GUIDE to an act of great generosity. The paintings shown in this building, which form perhaps the finest group of Early Renaissance pictures in the world, have been acquired – in most cases one by one – over a hundred and fifty years. We are now able to house them worthily, to keep them under proper conditions and, we hope, to make it easier for visitors to enjoy them to the full.

The site to the west of the National Gallery lay empty for forty-five years after its bombing in 1940, was long used as a car park, and only narrowly escaped development as a commercial office block. It now holds some of the most beautiful picture galleries built this century, as well as providing the lecture theatre, cinema, seminar rooms, shop and restaurant which gallery-goers world-wide today expect to find in a great national collection.

The Sainsbury Wing is named in honour of the three brothers – John, Simon and Timothy – who made possible this transformation. They have given this building to the nation and thus take their place among the greatest benefactors of the National Gallery since its foundation in 1824.

To them a large debt of gratitude is owed. This book, it is hoped, will sharpen our visitors' pleasure in looking at the Early Renaissance collection. May it also express our thanks to three outstanding friends of the National Gallery.

NEIL MacGREGOR
Director

Triptych: The Virgin and Child with Saints and Donors ('The Donne Triptych') (detail), c. 1475, by Hans Memlinc.

Introduction

OPPOSITE
The Sainsbury Wing from
Trafalgar Square.

BELOW
Lord Sainsbury of Preston Candover
(centre), Simon Sainsbury (left) and
Timothy Sainsbury MP (right).

THE COMPLETION of the Sainsbury Wing represents a dual achievement of major significance for London and indeed the entire country. On the one hand, it has contributed to the architecture of the capital, at its very centre, a world-class building, and a fitting neighbour to the monuments by Wilkins, Smirke and Gibbs which surround it. On the other, it has provided a new home for the nation's pictures, specifically for the great paintings of the Early Renaissance, the finest holding of its kind and one of the highlights of the National Gallery Collection. In both respects the new building represents a milestone in architecture: as a complex post-modern design conceived uniquely for its site, and as an unsurpassed space for pictures, heralding after decades of modernism a return to some of the best features of nineteenth-century museum architecture.

The birth of this great new gallery has not been painless, and the chequered history of its progress and setbacks has often been headline news. Since the bombing of Hampton's furniture store in 1940, the site has lain vacant, a gaping hole at the corner of London's most famous square, awaiting development. It was purchased by the Government in 1958 for the future expansion of the National Gallery, but no funds were subsequently forthcoming to build an extension. Various proposals came to nothing and in 1984 a competition for a commercially funded building ended in failure. The now infamous 'carbuncle on the face of a much-loved friend' was refused planning permission after a planning enquiry. It seemed that the problems of securing funding and achieving a design which would satisfy the demands of the site were insurmountable. But then in 1985 rescue came through the unprecedented generosity of the Sainsbury brothers, who offered to pay for a building entirely for the Gallery's use. The long history of delays and frustrations was reversed overnight and in only six years their gift has borne fruit in the splendid building now unveiled. New plans were formed, advice sought and within six months an architect, Robert Venturi of Philadelphia, was selected. In April 1987 his scheme was made public, and in January 1988 construction began. In three years the building was completed, on time and within budget, a most happy conclusion to a story begun in the dark days of the Second World War.

The significance of this gift to the nation can hardly be overestimated. The Sainsbury Wing galleries greatly increase the available space for pictures, and allow room for the growth of the Collection for many years to come. With the move of the Early Renaissance collection into the new galleries, space has been liberated in the old building for the later periods of painting, permitting the entire Collection once again to be on show, and allowing a completely new arrangement. The opening of the Sainsbury Wing inaugurates a radically new division of the Collection into four main areas: painting before 1510 in the Sainsbury Wing, and sixteenth-century painting, seventeenth-century painting, and painting after 1700 in the three 'wings' of the old building. This subdivision by period will help visitors to orientate themselves in the enlarged Gallery, to choose the part of the Collection they most wish to see, and to

comprehend more easily the historical context and significance of the paintings.

In addition to providing new galleries of the highest quality for the presentation of the Collection, the new building also includes space for temporary exhibitions, a large auditorium, a restaurant, a Gallery shop, a computerised information room and meeting rooms. As such it inaugurates a new era in the Gallery's history. The old building, built in several phases during the nineteenth and early twentieth centuries, has always lacked suitable space for the reception of large numbers of visitors. In recent decades, as museum-going has reached unprecedented popularity, the number of visitors has increased several fold, and now totals between three and four million a year. For many of these visitors the mute spectacle of the paintings is not in itself enough. There is a thirst for instruction, information and those facilities which make a museum or gallery a welcoming and comfortable place to visit. The lecture rooms, restaurants, and shops where books, postcards and souvenirs can be bought, are a necessary complement to the galleries of pictures and enhance the quality of the experience of viewing paintings. Now, within the new Sainsbury Wing, the Gallery is able to serve its visitors better than ever before. A fuller and richer menu of exhibitions, talks, films and conferences is now possible, appealing to visitors of all kinds and ages from the curious layman to the scholar, from schoolchild to seasoned art-lover.

Hampton's furniture store, Pall Mall East, after being gutted by a high explosive bomb in November 1940.

The Building of the Sainsbury Wing

FROM THE MOMENT that Lord Sainsbury of Preston Candover and his brothers, Simon and Timothy, announced in April 1985 their intention to fund a new building on the Hampton site, entirely for the Gallery's use, work began on a new architectural brief that would exploit the potential of the site to the full and specify in detail the requirements of the Gallery. The wish of the Gallery and the donors was that the new building should be devoted almost exclusively to public use.

New picture galleries were the chief requirement, but other public facilities were now added: the temporary exhibition galleries, the auditorium, the restaurant, the shop, the meeting rooms, and the Micro Gallery – an exciting proposal to provide computerised information on the Collection through interactive VDUs. In addition, it was decided that there should be a major new entrance on Trafalgar Square, to relieve congestion at the main Gallery entrance and to allow direct access to temporary exhibitions, lectures and other facilities in the new wing, possibly outside normal Gallery hours.

The Hampton site – so named after the store that stood there until 1940 – lies immediately to the west of the National Gallery, at the corner of Trafalgar Square on Pall Mall. It is a constricted irregular site bounded to the west and north by narrow streets, survivors of seventeenth-century London's layout, and to the east by a public footpath, Jubilee Walk, which separates it from the existing Gallery. It was early decided that this walkway should remain and that the extension should be a separate structure linked to the main building by a bridge at gallery level. It was also decided that the new galleries should be at the same level as those in the main building and should occupy the whole of the top floor

Map (dated 1894–6) of Trafalgar Square. The Hampton site, immediately to the west of the National Gallery, is a constricted irregular site bounded to the north and west by narrow streets and to the east by the public footpath Jubilee Walk.

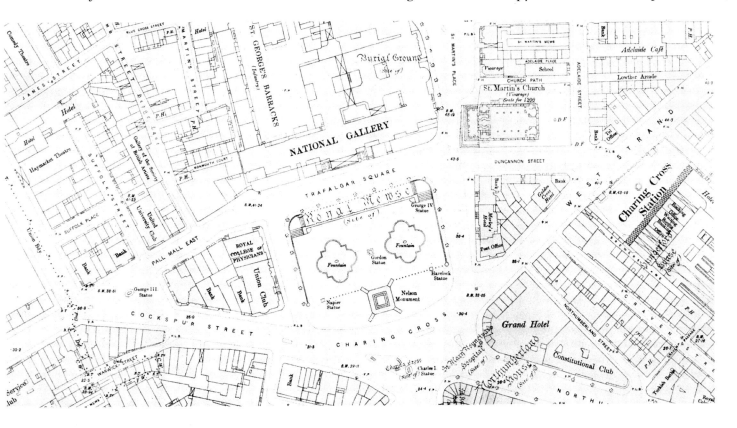

9

of the Sainsbury Wing, where they could most benefit from the available daylight.

While the brief was being compiled, the search began for an architect. In the course of six months many hundreds of names were considered, advice was sought, architects interviewed, and visits made to new buildings of note throughout the world. Two architectural advisers were appointed to help the Gallery Trustees and the donors in their search: Ada Louis Huxtable, former architectural correspondent for the *New York Times*, and Colin Amery, architectural correspondent for the *Financial Times*. With their help, a shortlist of six candidates was agreed comprising four British architects, Colquhoun and Miller, Jeremy Dixon with BDP, Piers Gough, and James Stirling, and two American, Henry Cobb and Robert Venturi. These six were asked to present initial proposals and on the basis of these, in January 1986, Robert Venturi was selected as architect of the new extension.

During the next year there followed an intensive process of research, discussion and design, involving architects, donors, Trustees, consultants and Gallery staff. A tour was organised of Italian galleries and sites – including the Accademia and the Museo di San Marco in Florence, the Brera, the Ambrosiana and the Castello Sforzesco in Milan, the Castelvecchio in Verona and museums in Venice, Siena and Ferrara – to

The basement area of the Sainsbury Wing during the early stages of construction with the secant piles still exposed.

From left to right: Lord Sainsbury, Lord Rothschild and Neil MacGregor, Director of the National Gallery, greeting Their Royal Highnesses The Prince and Princess of Wales at the laying of the foundation stone in March 1988.

see how paintings of a kind similar to those to be shown in the new wing are displayed in Italy. Finally, after much coming and going between Philadelphia and London and intensive discussions with the Gallery, Robert Venturi presented his scheme for the extension at the National Gallery in April 1987. Planning permission was granted and in January 1988, after an archeological dig had uncovered and recorded some of the gravel pits of Saxon London, construction commenced.

In order to carry out the building work and administer the project, a charitable company and an active subsidiary were formed, with Gallery Trustees and donors as directors and the property developer Stuart Lipton as adviser. In an effort to ensure speedy progress and tight cost control, it was decided to adopt the construction management method, whereby the client enters into separate contracts with the various trades associated with the project, and a Construction Manager – Sir Robert McAlpine Construction Management Ltd – was appointed to control and co-ordinate these trade contractors. Together, the client's Project Manager, Eric Gabriel, and the Construction Manager ensured that the input of the contractors was successfully dovetailed to produce a building of the highest quality.

The completion of the first stage of construction was marked by the laying of the foundation stone on 30 March 1988 by Their Royal Highnesses The Prince and Princess of Wales. This initial construction work followed an unconventional method. The perimeter retaining wall was formed by 256 secant piles which were cast deep into the London clay and stand in contact, thus forming a totally enclosing 'tank' that can withstand considerable pressure from the surrounding ground. Subsequently, the concrete slab for the ground floor was cast, securing the piles against lateral movement. Only then did the deep excavation work of the lower levels begin through the aperture of the basement stairwell; at the same time work began on the construction of the concrete shell of the building above ground. This extraordinary method speeded up construction by allowing work to proceed simultaneously above and below ground. As the earth was removed from below and the surrounding piles revealed, the illusion was created that this was indeed an archeological site, and that an immense buried structure of a former age was in the process of being uncovered.

By May 1989 the concrete and steel structure was complete, and the Topping Out ceremony was held in the as yet unpartitioned space of the gallery floor. Brickwork and stone cladding proceeded and the rooflights were installed so that by August the building was weathertight. Then began the complex internal finishing, which involved stonemasons, carpenters and decorators working closely alongside mechanical and electrical contractors.

A formidable array of materials has been gathered from around the world to form and embellish this remarkable building: Portland stone from Dorset, limestone from Chamesson, France, silver grey slate from Cumbria, pietra serena from Tuscany, black granite from Minnesota, specially made bricks from Leicester, and white oak flooring from

The Architect – Robert Venturi

ROBERT VENTURI was selected as architect of the Sainsbury Wing from an international field. From the first the Trustees and donors were struck by his concern for context – in this case the difficult and demanding context of Trafalgar Square – and his wish that the 'galleries should be rooms for looking at paintings in, not contraptions for containing them' – a view very much in accordance with that of the Gallery staff and Trustees. His initial proposals contained all the essential elements of the final design – the inflected façade with its classical detailing used in an unconventional manner, the grand, glazed staircase, reminiscent of an Italian external staircase, and the three parallel ranges of lofty, dignified galleries – and it was these, and his assurance that he would work closely with the Gallery, that won him this major commission.

Venturi was born in 1925 in Philadelphia and trained at Princeton University School of Architecture. In 1954 he won the Rome Prize (a leading prize for American architectural students), which enabled him to study for two years at the American Academy in Italy. On his return he worked for Eero Saarinen and Louis Kahn and then taught at the universities of Pennsylvania and Yale. In 1964 he formed a partnership with John Rauch, which his wife, Denise Scott Brown, joined in 1967.

It is in his writings, and particularly in his book *Complexity and Contradiction in Architecture*, published in 1966, that he has had most influence, advocating a richer and more allusive architecture that derives its validity from diversity and depth of meaning. In his design for the

ABOVE
Robert Venturi.

RIGHT
Robert Venturi (right) and Denise Scott Brown descending the external staircase at the Certosa di Galuzzo near Florence, during a tour of Italian museums and galleries in 1986.

LEFT
Gordon Wu Hall, Butler College,
completed in 1983, one of several
buildings at Princeton University
designed by Robert Venturi.

Sainsbury Wing we see that ambition realised in a building which in part echoes its neighbours, and which internally evokes the grand spaces of Italian palazzi and English country houses.

Venturi also had valuable experience of working on museum projects. In 1973 his firm had added a wing to the Allen Memorial Art Museum at Oberlin College, Ohio, and at the time of his selection he was working on three other museum buildings – the Seattle Art Museum, the Laguna Gloria Museum in Austin, Texas, and the Contemporary Art Museum at La Jolla, California. While he had never had to work with a collection of such importance as the National Gallery's, he was well aware of the problems of accommodating large numbers of visitors without over-whelming the paintings; of meeting the complex environmental needs of the pictures without turning the galleries into machines; and of fitting in all the other facilities required in a twentieth-century museum, such as restaurants, lecture theatres, bookshops and information services. As he said:

> While our ideal is to produce galleries that are architecturally analo-gous to the aesthetic of the paintings displayed in them and familiar, conventional, and even perhaps traditional in their forms and the associations they evoke, our spaces must also be of their own time, and must of course be workable, and must maintain stringent tech-nical and aesthetic standards that are current for lighting and environmental quality – not to mention standards that are appropri-ate to the crowds that attend today's museums.

BELOW
A sketch by the architect for the
Sainsbury Wing galleries showing
the diminishing perspective.

America. The roof glazing is from Austria and Switzerland, sunblinds from England, glazed curtain walling from Holland and Belgium, lighting from Germany, ceiling tiles from Switzerland, carpets from Kidderminster and America, and lifts from Japan. With consultants, contractors and suppliers from around the world this is truly an international building, designed to contain a collection of world-wide importance, and to receive visitors of all nationalities.

The construction of the Sainsbury Wing was completed by the end of 1990, and following the commissioning and testing of the air conditioning and other services the pictures were moved in. Occupied and open to the public it now ceases to be an isolated structure and begins its life as the Sainsbury Wing of the National Gallery.

OPPOSITE
Nelson's Column seen from the grand staircase of the Sainsbury Wing.

BELOW
The Gallery from New Zealand House, showing in the foreground the roof of the Sainsbury Wing under construction. INSET Two masons working on the interior stonework.

WILLIAM WILKINS'S National Gallery, opened in 1838, spans the entire north side of Trafalgar Square. Classical in style, it is symmetrical in design and has at its centre a portico supported by Corinthian columns. Robert Venturi's building was conceived as a complement to this classical façade, a separate but connected extension, which defers to the old building. It is an asymmetrical building, a fragment which depends upon the old building for its meaning and function. Standing at the corner of Trafalgar Square, its eccentric shape, evident both from the outside and from the interior spaces, is determined by the geometry of the surrounding streets, and its entrance façade inflects towards the square and Wilkins's National Gallery.

This deferential character is reflected too in the detailed design of the façade. Venturi's extension is the same height as Wilkins's building, and is also faced with Portland stone. On the east end of the façade clustered pilasters and blind window reveals echo its neighbour, but further west these classical elements diminish until, as the façade meets Whitcomb Street, it has become an unornamented wall of stone. This essentially different character is reflected too in the entrance, which in contrast to the projecting elevated portico of the main building is a recessed opening cut into the façade. Leading directly from the pavement, it eschews the dignified associations of the main entrance and invites easy access. The

A Tour of the Building

Venturi meets Wilkins. The main façade of the National Gallery with the Sainsbury Wing on the left.

Jubilee Walk. The new wing is linked to the main building by a circular bridge.

One of the new capitals, copied from those on the main building.

inflective character of the extension and its dependence on its context are similarly evident in its other aspects: the high window on Pall Mall, suggestive of others on this grand street, the brick elevation on Whitcomb Street, mirroring the walls opposite, and the unadorned rear elevation, broken only by the large stone panel announcing in monumental incised lettering the identity of the building to pedestrians arriving from Leicester Square.

The east wall, facing the National Gallery across Jubilee Walk, is different again. This huge glass curtain wall, so unlike the entrance façade, allows passers-by to glimpse inside the building to the great staircase leading to the galleries and to the inner fenestrated stone wall which does indeed echo the west elevation of Wilkins's building on the opposite side of the walkway. The effect is to make the staircase seem like a monumental exterior staircase, rising up between twin façades.

This layering of the building is repeated at the front, an inner glass wall becoming visible behind the stone screen of the entrance and a second interior wall rising up behind the Pall Mall window. In this way Venturi hints at the dual purpose of the architecture: to provide an external envelope dictated by the urban context and especially the neoclassical architecture of the square, and an inner shell to contain the Gallery's Collection, determined by the complex needs of the paintings.

Carving the frieze of artists' names on the inner stone wall of the grand staircase.

Two views of the grand staircase with its monumental frieze of artists' names.

Passing through the entrance doors, the visitor enters into a large hall extending far inside. Seemingly oversized for such a building, this entrance hall is designed to receive a large proportion of the Gallery's visitors, its function thus relating to both buildings. Like the hall of an English country house or Italian villa it is a stony space with a patterned slate floor and Chamesson limestone walls, and is lower than the principal rooms on the top floor. The wall bordering the staircase to the right is heavily rusticated and at intervals throughout the hall are massive stone piers and columns, emphasising its crypt-like character. The entrance is irregular in plan, however, with a curved wall leading to the information desk and cloakroom, and beyond these to the lifts and the staircase to the lower floors.

Immediately apparent on the left is the entrance to the Gallery shop, which is separated from the entrance hall by a glazed screen wall and a row of decorative cast-iron pillars. The shop, which was designed by McIlroy Coates of Edinburgh, is finished in American oak. It has windows overlooking Whitcomb Street and a separate entrance at the corner of Pall Mall and Whitcomb Street. It is one of the largest retail developments of any European museum or gallery, holding an extensive selection of books and a large range of Gallery products.

To the right of the entrance hall the visitor is drawn to the foot of the grand staircase, which after the low horizontal space of the entrance is one of the great architectural surprises of the building. Flooded by light from the huge glazed east wall, this lofty staircase rises in one flight of over 35 metres to the picture galleries on the top floor. On the left rises the inner stone wall pierced by openings at first floor level and large windows at the gallery level and bearing a monumental frieze of Renaissance artists' names, incised by the letter carver Michael Harvey. Despite its grandeur, the staircase like the rest of the building does not conform to tradition. It is asymmetrical, rising to one side of the building, and widening as it ascends. Suspended above it are decorative iron arches, which emphasise its external character and are reminiscent of the nineteenth-century industrial architecture of Paxton and his contemporaries.

A similar staircase descends to the lower floors from the rear of the entrance hall, immediately below the grand staircase. Behind these stairs are the two passenger lifts serving all five levels. The vertical circulation is therefore concentrated along the east flank of the building. On all levels below the main galleries a secondary circulation space runs parallel to the stairs. The staircase thus provides the visitor with a strong reference point, ensuring that the layout of the building is clear and comprehensible at all times.

Descending the lower staircase from the rear of the entrance hall, the visitor comes to a half landing which opens onto the lower ground floor. Here are situated the lecture theatre and the main toilets. A small lobby, surrounded by bench seats and clad in dark blue boarding, serves as a foyer to the theatre, which is gently raked and can seat 340 persons. It is divided into front and rear areas, so that small audiences can comfortably

occupy the front rows. At the rear is the projection suite, which includes video and slide-projection equipment, sound systems, and a translation booth for conference use. The stage is designed primarily for lectures and slide projection, but can also accommodate conference platforms and small-scale musical and dramatic performances. This auditorium is now the Gallery's chief lecture theatre, and has made possible a more ambitious programme of events than hitherto, including specialist art-related conferences, and advertised talks by celebrated speakers.

Continuing down the lower staircase the visitor arrives at the basement level, which houses the temporary exhibition galleries. At the foot of the staircase is a lofty circular foyer, paved in slate, with to one side an oak-topped catalogue sales desk. To the right is the cinema, a fan-shaped room with back-projection facilities for showing videos and tape-slide programmes in conjunction with temporary exhibitions. Bench seats provide seating for about fifty people with standing room at the rear.

The temporary exhibition space measures about 500 square metres and is divided into six galleries, which lead off the circular foyer. They have

ABOVE
The bottom of the lower staircase leading from the basement to the ground floor.

OPPOSITE ABOVE
The circular foyer to the temporary exhibition galleries.

OPPOSITE
The lecture theatre on the lower ground floor.

painted plaster walls, oak floors and painted timber skirtings and archi-traves. The rooms are of varying size and height, and are separated by sliding doors so that they can be used in different combinations accord-ing to the requirements of individual exhibitions, and so that rooms can be easily closed off if not required. The galleries have a flexible light-track lighting system and can be used with the minimum of installation, thus reducing costs. On this level also are changing rooms and rest rooms for staff, and exhibition support areas – a packing room and storage for pictures and cases. A large service lift allows works of art to be moved easily between floors.

Returning to the entrance hall, the visitor reaches the first floor from a landing halfway up the grand staircase. Here are situated the restaurant, the computer information room and meeting rooms. The restaurant occupies the front of the building and is a low irregular space with floor-to-ceiling windows which look across the covered entrance arcade through the massive openings of the façade towards Trafalgar Square. At the far side the ceiling suddenly and unexpectedly rises to reveal the tall window on Pall Mall and a shaft-like space overhead which separates the external wall and the inner wall of the galleries. The detailing of the room is typically fine, with a decorative painted dado rail and an oak-topped coffee bar with handsome glazed cabinets behind. On the west

wall are three large pictures, specially painted for the room by Paula Rego, the themes of which derive from the Early Renaissance collection displayed on the main floor.

The Micro Gallery computer information room is situated in a long narrow room with windows onto Whitcomb Street. Along one side are work stations incorporating computer terminals. The specially developed computer system, funded by the American Express Foundation, enables visitors to call up onto the screen images of pictures in the Collection, together with information about them and the artists who

ABOVE
The fan-shaped cinema off the exhibitions foyer at basement level.

LEFT
The restaurant overlooking Pall Mall East and Trafalgar Square.

ON THE WEST WALL of the new restaurant of the Sainsbury Wing hang three large paintings by the artist Paula Rego, which have been painted specially for this location. They stem from Paula's close involvement with the Gallery and its Collection. In 1990 she became the first National Gallery Associate Artist, a new appointment intended to give an established artist the opportunity of working in the Gallery and of producing work directly related to paintings in the Collection.

Paula's work is richly allusive, drawing extensively on people and events from legend as well as on her own life and imagination. When she was asked to paint what is in effect a large mural for the Sainsbury Wing restaurant, she decided to draw her themes from the lives of the saints as told in *The Golden Legend* and as represented in many of the Early Renaissance pictures hanging in the new galleries. Her cast of characters is brought together in one fictional place, the garden of the fifteenth-century Italian painter Carlo Crivelli.

Her pictures are full of detail and incident and repay long study. Several features, however, immediately bring to mind the early paintings from which they derive – the oddities of perspective, for example, and the conflicting scale of the figures. Several stories are represented in each picture, and, as in medieval paintings, the same character may appear more than once to tell a narrative. Some stories are represented in friezes of images on the walls of buildings, intended as decorative ceramic wall-tiles, a common feature in Paula's native Portugal.

Crivelli's Garden
by Paula Rego

BELOW
Crivelli's Garden (The Visitation)
(detail). Acrylic on canvas.

LEFT
Paula Rego in her National Gallery studio with one of the paintings from the *Crivelli's Garden* series.

The Micro Gallery

THE MICRO GALLERY Computer Information Room, sponsored by the American Express Foundation, provides a facility which enables visitors to find out more about the Collection and to explore it in new ways.

The room contains fourteen computer terminals, each comprising a colour 'touch screen' whereby the visitor selects the information of interest by touching appropriate choices on the screen. The system is simple to operate and provides a rich and interesting insight into the Collection.

The system contains a complete catalogue of the Gallery's Collection of over 2,200 paintings, life histories of the artists, an illustrated historical atlas of European art, an illustrated glossary and a subject index. Presented in the style of a good art book, it provides serious yet non-specialist information in a highly visual and accessible way, combining text and high-resolution picture reproductions with graphics and animated sequences.

The information in the system is interconnected to allow the visitor to browse freely, moving from an artist's biography to his paintings, or from a painting to another on the same subject, or from a painting to an article about its restoration. The user can look up specific pictures, or determine which works on a given subject are to be found in the Gallery. Alternatively, visitors can follow themes in painting, e.g. portraits, look up historical information, or take a 'guided tour' that gives information about a chosen set of paintings.

A 'page' from the Micro Gallery, with text and colour images from the Collection combined on the computer screen. Print-outs can be requested of any information displayed, including personalised guide maps indicating the location of chosen paintings. The printers are controlled by electronic cards, similar to phonecards, purchased from special dispensers in the room.

□ *Virgin and Child* CIMA

□ *The Madonna of the Meadow* Giovanni BELLINI

□ *Virgin and Child with Goldfinch* CIMA

Bellini influenced many Venetian painters, including Titian and Giorgione. Cima was active in Venice 1492 to 1516 and particularly shows Bellini's influence in pictures of the Virgin and Child.

Cima uses Bellini's parapet motif to separate the holy figures from us, the earthly viewers. The tender mother-child image owes much to Bellini. Cima also echoes Bellini's colouring and use of background landscapes.

ABOVE
The link bridge on the main floor
with the new doorway opening into
the old galleries.

BELOW
The finely crafted pietra serena
stonework of the main floor
galleries.

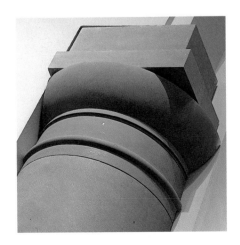

painted them. Also on this floor, bordering Whitcomb Street, is a series of three meeting rooms, equipped with audio-visual facilities. These are available for use by special groups for talks, seminars and receptions.

Continuing up the main staircase the visitor arrives on the main floor. This landing is the fulcrum of the Sainsbury Wing, where the staircase, the link with the main building, the lifts and the entrance to the new galleries converge. To the right a broad stone-paved passage leads across a circular bridge above Jubilee Walk to the galleries in the main building. The bridge is glazed on either side, its curved full-length windows looking south towards the square and north towards a new garden planted with plane trees. To the left of the staircase a vista of receding arched openings, flanked by pietra serena columns and terminating in Cima's altarpiece of *The Incredulity of Saint Thomas*, leads into the magnificent new galleries. The openings diminish in size, forming a false perspective and giving an impression of increased distance.

The galleries were conceived specifically for the Early Renaissance collection, which comprises Northern and Italian works painted before 1510. The size of these pictures varies enormously, from large altarpieces four metres and more in height, to small portraits and devotional works of only a few centimetres. It was clearly desirable to have rooms of varying size and height, appropriate to the pictures. Robert Venturi therefore designed the galleries in three ranges of rooms running the length of the building from north to south. The central range is the loftiest with walls 5.5 metres high. Most of the galleries of the eastern range have walls 5 metres high, while those of the western range are 4.5 metres. The central range provides a nave-like spine to the building, and consists of four rooms linked by broad arched openings in an enfilade reminiscent of Sir John Soane's Dulwich Picture Gallery. The visitor can see the extent of these central galleries at a glance, the vista being dramatically terminated at each end by an altarpiece. The central range is crossed at three points by vistas extending east and west across the building into the side rooms, thus giving a sense of the galleries' breadth.

In contrast, the connecting doors in the side galleries are not aligned, to strike a more informal note and to encourage the visitor to linger and take in each room and its contents. Four of the rooms on the east side have windows that look out across the grand staircase to the glazed east wall and the main building beyond.

The layout of the new galleries is both lucid and reassuring. It is impossible to get lost in these rooms, and there is a sense of ceremony and procession, particularly in the central spaces, which is appropriate for the paintings and seldom found in modern galleries.

While the rooms vary in size and geometry, the general design and character are homogeneous. Nearly all the rooms have skirtings and door casings of pietra serena (the grey Italian sandstone favoured by Renaissance architects), oak floors with stone surrounds, and grey plaster walls. Throughout are simple wooden benches designed by the British furniture designer Martin Grierson, who also designed the seats for the entrance hall and landings. The effect is uniformly serene and dignified, reminiscent of the churches and palaces from which many of the paintings once came. This is reinforced by the ceiling design. The galleries rise to a great height with heavy moulded cornices, steeply sloping covings and high clerestory windows. The ceilings and covings are made of an acoustic material to temper the reverberation of the hard spaces.

A particularly beautiful quality of the galleries is the light which filters down from a great height and subtly changes with the day. All the galleries, excepting a small room designed for the Leonardo Cartoon, are lit by daylight, which enters laterally through the clerestory windows. Beyond these windows are glazed roof spaces containing movable sun louvres and giving access to air-conditioning duct-work. The louvres cut out direct sunlight and reduce the general quantity of light when necessary to levels that conform to conservation standards. Nevertheless, the light entering the galleries is still directional, and the position of the sun and changes in the weather are evident in the galleries, giving them a 'live', natural quality.

The electric lighting is located high in the ceilings, and consists of low-voltage tungsten-halogen lamps with special lenses to spread the light evenly across the walls. Some of these are in constant use, supplementing the daylight. Others automatically come on as the daylight fails.

The lighting strategy was developed by the American lighting consultant Paul Marantz in response to the Gallery's brief for controlled but variable daylight. During the design phase, a full-scale mock-up of a gallery was built at Shepperton Film Studios to enable the lighting design to be exhaustively tested. For a year tests were carried out with the actual lights and blinds proposed for the galleries, and old framed copies of National Gallery pictures hung on the walls to simulate gallery conditions as closely as possible. It was not only possible to measure changing light levels in the mock-up, but also to make subjective judgements about light effects.

The careful control of light levels and the elimination of ultra-violet light represent only one aspect of the complex environmental control required for the paintings now housed in the new galleries. These pictures are the oldest in the Collection, and are especially vulnerable to climatic change. Nearly all are painted on panels of wood, which predated canvas as the most popular support for paintings. These wooden panels hold a certain amount of water, and depending on the moisture level of the surrounding air will absorb or give out water, expanding and contracting as they do so. Such changes can have disastrous effects, resulting in warping and even splitting of the wood, and damage to the paint surface. For this reason it is essential that the humidity of the galleries in which such paintings are hung is kept stable by air conditioning.

All those parts of the new building designed to accommodate paintings are fully air-conditioned, and the humidity and lighting are automatically controlled by a computerised building management system. It is this technology, invisible to the casual visitor, which ensures the safe preservation of the paintings.

ABOVE
The diminishing perspective to the left of the grand staircase, terminating in *The Incredulity of Saint Thomas, c.* 1504, by Cima.

OPPOSITE
The central galleries, looking north, with *The Crucified Christ, c.* 1503, by Raphael.

BELOW
The enfilade of galleries at Sir John Soane's Dulwich Picture Gallery.

THE COLLECTION of late medieval and Early Renaissance paintings at the National Gallery is probably the finest and most representative of its kind in the world. It contains masterpieces which have come to be regarded as among the very highest achievements in painting of any period, and which are familiar to all lovers of art – paintings such as Uccello's *Battle of San Romano*, van Eyck's *'Arnolfini Marriage'*, Piero della Francesca's *Baptism of Christ*, Bellini's *Doge Leonardo Loredan* and Leonardo's *Virgin of the Rocks*. It is unusual in having outstanding groups of both Italian and Northern paintings, and one of the aims of the new display has been to show these groups in closer conjunction than ever before. Rather than being separated into national schools, the paintings have been integrated in a chronological arrangement, to emphasise the relationships between Italian and Northern painting in the fifteenth century and to allow new comparisons to be made. Masaccio and the artists of the Early Italian Renaissance are now hung close to Campin, van Eyck and Rogier van der Weyden, who were working in the same years in the Netherlands; Antonello da Messina is near to Bouts and Memlinc; and the late fifteenth-century masters, Bellini, Cima, Costa, Perugino and Raphael, are close to their Northern contemporaries, Gerard David, Massys and Dürer. Only with a collection as representative of Northern and Italian painting as this can such conjunctions be achieved.

The wealth of this part of the Collection is due in no small measure to the energy and far-sightedness of Charles Locke Eastlake, the Gallery's

The Early Renaissance Collection

The Battle of San Romano, c. 1450s, by Paolo Uccello.

ABOVE
'The Arnolfini Marriage',
1434, by Jan van Eyck.

BELOW
Sir Charles Locke Eastlake, Director
of the National Gallery 1855–65.

first Director, and his successors William Boxall and Frederic William Burton, who during the second half of the nineteenth century travelled extensively in Europe acquiring paintings – often for negligible sums. Before Eastlake became Director in 1855, the early schools had been neglected in favour of sixteenth- and seventeenth-century painting. For the first thirty years of the Gallery's history, from its foundation in 1824, purchases were made in an ad hoc manner by the Trustees or by the Government. The prevailing taste was conservative. Sir Robert Peel, who became a Trustee in 1827, was opposed to the purchase of early Italian works, regarding them as 'curiosities', while another Trustee, Lord Aberdeen, strongly objected to the purchase of what he termed 'antiquarian and medieval pictures'. The narrow views of the Trustees, and attempts at cleaning the pictures, came under public attack in 1846 and 1847 by, among others, the young John Ruskin. Writing in *The Times*, he accused the Trustees of 'cumbering our walls with pictures that have no single virtue, no colour, no drawing, no character, no history, no thought,' and of failing to acquire any works by such artists as Perugino, Fra Angelico, Fra Bartolommeo, Verrocchio and Lorenzo di Credi. In 1853 the painter William Dyce, an early champion of the primitives, joined the fray in a letter to Prince Albert, who had shown himself to be far in advance of current ideas in his appreciation of the Early Renaissance both in Italy and the North. Dyce stressed the entire want of system in the Trustees' management of the Collection and their failure to see that the formation of a national collection demanded a methodical and catholic survey of the whole field of painting.

In response to mounting pressure, the House of Commons in 1853 appointed a Select Committee to inquire into the affairs of the Gallery. The Report of the Committee recommended that the scope of purchases should be widened and should include the early masters: 'What Chaucer and Spenser are to Shakespeare and Milton, Giotto and Masaccio are to the great masters of the Florentine School.' The constitution of the Gallery was revised, and Charles Locke Eastlake, President of the Royal Academy and former Keeper of the Gallery, was appointed as the first Director, with responsibility for acquiring paintings.

Before the mid-century, painting prior to 1500 was scarcely represented in the Collection at all. Two remarkable exceptions were van Eyck's *'Arnolfini Marriage'*, purchased in 1842, and Bellini's *Doge Leonardo Loredan*, bought in 1844, each for £630, a very modest sum in comparison with prices paid for later paintings. The first early Italian paintings to enter the Collection were two panels depicting saints by Lorenzo Monaco, given in 1848, to which was added in 1902 the central panel of the same altarpiece, *The Coronation of the Virgin*. And in 1854, on the advice of Dyce, the Chancellor of the Exchequer bought the Krüger Collection at Minden, which formed the basis of the representation of German painting before 1500.

The imbalance was rapidly corrected by Eastlake who in his ten years as Director regularly travelled in Italy and Europe purchasing works of the highest order, thus transforming the National Gallery in a few years

Queen Victoria's Gift

IN 1863, following the death of Prince Albert, Queen Victoria presented twenty-five paintings to the National Gallery 'in fulfilment of the wishes of His Royal Highness the Prince Consort'. These pictures were the best of a collection of Byzantine and early German, Netherlandish and Italian paintings which Prince Albert had acquired in 1851 from Prince Ludwig of Oettingen Wallerstein. Prince Louis had offered them to Prince Albert as security for a loan of £3,000 which he was later unable to repay. Apparently it was Prince Albert's intention from the first to present the finest of them to the National Gallery, thus enhancing its negligible early collections, but it was only after his death that his wish was fulfilled by Queen Victoria's Gift.

The most outstanding of the group are certainly the fifteenth-century German paintings, particularly the *Saints Peter and Dorothy* by the Master of the Saint Bartholomew Altarpiece, *The Presentation in the Temple* by the Master of the Life of the Virgin, and *Saints Matthew, Catherine of Alexandria and John the Evangelist* by Stephan Lochner. Of the Netherlandish paintings the finest are the beautiful Studio of Memlinc *Virgin and Child* and Gerard David's *Ecclesiastic Praying*. Later in date, and therefore not shown in the Sainsbury Wing, is the intriguing *Saint Christopher carrying the Infant Christ* in the style of the Master of the Female Half-Lengths, with its extensive landscape reminiscent of Pieter Brueghel. The outstanding Italian picture is the *Triptych: The Coronation of the Virgin* by Giusto de' Menabuoi, which is also the earliest of the pictures in the group, being signed and dated 1367. It is beautifully preserved and shows the Virgin crowned by Christ, with, on the inside of the shutters, the Annunciation, the Nativity and the Crucifixion, and, on the outside of the shutters, scenes from the life of the Virgin.

Prince Albert was a passionate collector of paintings, old and modern, and did much to foster the arts in Britain. In the 1840s, he acquired many early paintings for the Royal Collection, including a triptych by Duccio, and the *Madonna and Child with Angels* by Gentile de Fabriano (on loan to the National Gallery and on show in the Sainsbury Wing galleries), at a time when they were still unfashionable. His was the inspiration behind the fresco paintings in the Houses of Parliament, and he was the principal promoter of the hugely successful Great Exhibition of 1851. He was also largely responsible for the exhibition of 'Art Treasures of the United Kingdom' at Manchester in 1857, to which he and the Queen lent over a hundred paintings.

Prince Albert even submitted in 1853 his own proposals for the arrangement of the pictures in the National Gallery 'so as to afford the best means of instruction and education in the art to those who wish to

LEFT
Saints Peter and Dorothy, c. 1505–10,
by the Master of the Saint
Bartholomew Altarpiece.

ABOVE LEFT
Saints Matthew, Catherine of
Alexandria and John the Evangelist,
c. 1445, by Stephan Lochner.

study it scientifically in its history and progress,' thus clearly demonstrating his commitment to public education through the arts. Thereafter a more historical approach to the Collection was adopted.

Triptych: The Coronation of the Virgin, and other Scenes, 1367, by Giusto de' Menabuoi.

into one of the greatest collections of Early Renaissance painting. In 1855 he purchased works by Botticelli, Bellini and Mantegna; in 1856 the superb Perugino triptych of *The Virgin and Child; Saint Michael; Saint Raphael* and the Pollaiuolo brothers' *Martyrdom of Saint Sebastian* altarpiece; and in 1857 twenty-two works from the Lombardi-Baldi Collection in Florence, including works by Duccio, Segna, Orcagna, Niccolò di Pietro Gerini, Zoppo, the San Pier Maggiore altarpiece by Jacopo di Cione and, most notable of all, Paolo Uccello's *Battle of San Romano*. The following years brought more astonishing coups: Bellini's *Madonna of the Meadow* and Cossa's *Saint Vincent Ferrer* in 1858; two portraits by Campin and Rogier van der Weyden's *Magdalen Reading* from the Beaucousin Collection, and Bouts's *Entombment* in 1860; and in 1861 Piero della Francesca's *Baptism of Christ*, which was purchased at the Uzielli sale for only £241. Another purchase of that year was Fra Filippo Lippi's *Seven Saints*, which prompted Eastlake himself to present its companion, *The Annunciation*. In 1862 came Piero di Cosimo's *A Mythological Subject*, and in 1863 Bellini's *Agony in the Garden*. In this year, too, Queen Victoria presented to the nation, in fulfilment of the wishes of the Prince Consort, twenty-five paintings from the collection of Prince Ludwig of Oettingen Wallerstein. These early German, Netherlandish and Italian works included the superb *Saints Peter and Dorothy* by the Master of the Saint Bartholomew Altarpiece.

The Magdalen Reading, c. 1440–50, by Rogier van der Weyden.

The remarkable influx of early masterpieces continued, albeit at a slower rate, under the directorships of Eastlake's successors, Boxall and Burton. From Eastlake's own collection came a group of Italian and Northern works, among them Bouts's *Virgin and Child with Saints Peter and Paul*, while Lady Eastlake presented Pisanello's *Virgin and Child with Saints George and Anthony Abbot*. Boxall also acquired Crivelli's imposing *Demidoff Altarpiece*, and Cima's *The Incredulity of Saint Thomas*, both of which occupy prominent positions in the Sainsbury Wing. Burton, whose directorship lasted until 1894, purchased the Piero *Nativity*, Botticelli's *Venus and Mars* and works by the Vivarini, Tura and Crivelli from the Alexander Barker sale in 1874, and two great Botticellis from the Fuller Maitland Collection in 1878. In 1880 he bought Leonardo's *Virgin of the Rocks*; in 1883 two panels from Duccio's *Maestà* altarpiece, Antonello's *Portrait of a Man* and Mantegna's *Samson and Delilah*; and in 1884 Raphael's *Ansidei Altarpiece*.

The acquisition of early paintings in these decades was not made at the expense of other periods. It was altogether a great age of collecting which saw the National Gallery emerge as one of the richest and most comprehensive holdings of European painting anywhere. Nevertheless, the greatest transformation was undoubtedly in the Early Renaissance collection and particularly in Italian quattrocento painting. In only a few decades the National Gallery rose to a position it has since retained, as having an early Italian collection unmatched outside Italy as well as a superb, albeit smaller, representation of Netherlandish and German painting.

Designing the New Galleries

FROM THE MOMENT that the planning of the new extension began, it was decided that the galleries should be used to show the early paintings. Rather than attempting to create spaces that would suit pictures of any period, and as a result possibly suit none especially well, it was agreed to design the galleries for specific works. Several factors determined that these should be the Early Renaissance paintings. Firstly, they are of a number that could be well accommodated in the available space. The opportunities for acquiring more prime examples of this period are limited, and it is not expected that the Early Renaissance collection will grow appreciably in the years to come. Secondly, it was felt that of all the schools and periods of painting represented in the Collection, this group was least well served by the existing galleries. Excepting the bland spaces of the north extension, built in the early 1970s, these galleries are chiefly nineteenth-century in origin and classical in style, with marble door cases and skirtings, and heavily moulded plasterwork ceilings. Their architecture is loosely derived from Italianate picture galleries of the sixteenth and seventeenth centuries and provides a grand setting for most styles of painting of these periods and later. Even the Impressionist and Post-Impressionist paintings, which are roughly contemporaneous with many of the galleries, look well in them. The paintings of the fifteenth century and earlier, however, were originally seen in settings of a very different kind. Most were painted for medieval churches and palaces, and were rarely collected when the concept of the picture gallery as we know it first developed in sixteenth-century Italy. More than most kinds of painting, their function was intimately connected with the buildings for which they were painted, and they suffer most in being removed from them. It seemed worthwhile, therefore, to try to create new galleries which, while not attempting to simulate the original settings of the paintings, would be more suitable in scale and character than the existing galleries.

Room 9, the Wohl Room. One of the recently restored galleries in the main building, containing sixteenth-century Venetian paintings.

View of Room 66 with
The Baptism of Christ,
1450s, by Piero della Francesca.

A third consideration was the wish to present a broadly chronological display. By placing the earliest pictures in the new wing at the western extremity of the Gallery, the chronology could unfold eastwards, culminating in the works of around 1900 in the east wing. Lastly, allocating the earliest pictures to the new galleries would ensure that these delicate panel paintings would benefit from the most up-to-date environmental control.

Since it had been decided which pictures the new galleries should house, it was possible to be specific about the kind of galleries that were needed and their arrangement. Above all, rooms of a conventional character were required, rather than the free-flowing space of many modern galleries, so that the pictures could be seen without distraction in spaces that appeared permanent, tranquil and dignified. Flexibility – in the sense of movable partitions and screens – was rejected. Instead, it was decided to aim for the best possible galleries for the pictures in question, in terms of scale, finish and lighting.

This decision immediately gave rise to questions about what sort of rooms and which materials were most suitable. The paintings themselves were originally housed in many different kinds of building – domestic and public, ecclesiastical and secular, classical and gothic, Italian and Northern. To recreate a period setting – even were it thought desirable – would therefore be impossible. The rooms had first and foremost to be picture galleries and to accommodate both paintings and visitors. Nevertheless, by judicious design and choice of materials it would be possible to produce an atmosphere which would enhance the paintings. It was decided to use chiefly hard materials – plaster, stone and timber – to emulate the solidity of medieval and Renaissance buildings and to act as a foil to the rich colouring and gilt frames of the paintings. The austerity of the finishes would also contrast with the elaborate architecture of the old building, with its marble, decorative plasterwork and patterned damask wall-hangings.

The layout of the rooms evolved in response to the proposed arrangement of the paintings – the 'ideal' hang. Their size and sequence were determined largely by the Collection itself, so that the pictures could be accommodated in their appropriate art-historical groupings, reflecting the particular nature of the Collection as it had evolved since the Gallery was founded. For example, some rooms were conceived for the work of specific artists, such as Piero and Botticelli, in which the Collection is particularly strong, others for regional schools – Netherlandish, German, Venetian, Florentine, etc. Smaller rooms with lower walls and ceilings were created for the smaller paintings, particularly the Netherlandish pictures, while the largest and loftiest rooms were reserved for the later Italian pictures, among which are a high proportion of large altarpieces. A further consideration was the wish to give emphasis to key exhibits: such pictures as *The Wilton Diptych*, 'The Arnolfini Marriage', Piero's *Baptism of Christ*, Cima's *Incredulity of Saint Thomas*, Raphael's *Crucified Christ* and Leonardo's *Virgin of the Rocks* all occupy conspicuous positions, chiefly at the end of vistas, enabling them to be seen and recognised at a distance.

As a tool to help refine the hang and to consider detailed questions of placing, a 1:20 scale model of the gallery floor was made, together with scale photographs of the 250 or so paintings. For months the curators worked with 'the doll's house' as it came to be known, shifting pictures and trying new juxtapositions before arriving at a more or less definitive arrangement. This exercise ensured that there were no protracted delays when the movement of these delicate works actually took place, and the final hang was achieved with the minimum of risk and effort.

The Director and curators discussing the arrangement of pictures in 'the doll's house' prior to hanging the paintings in the new galleries.

Preparing the Paintings

WHILE THE NEW BUILDING was taking shape, work was in progress out of the public eye in the Gallery's conservation and framing studios on the preparation of the pictures for display in the Sainsbury Wing galleries.

The 250 or so Early Renaissance paintings are the oldest in the Collection and among the most fragile. The majority are painted on wooden panels, many of which have suffered the ravages of time. Religious paintings have been displaced from their original settings, dismembered and sold, often surviving only as fragments, and many damaged works suffered again long ago at the hands of incompetent restorers.

Today great care and scientific skills are combined in the preservation and treatment of these works. Every one of the paintings hanging in the wing has been closely examined, and many have been treated in preparation for the hang. Over a period of six years, Jacopo di Cione's great San Pier Maggiore altarpiece has been painstakingly cleaned and restored. Other paintings to have been cleaned recently include Tura's *Allegorical Figure*, the Master of Moulins's *Meeting at the Golden Gate* and Crivelli's *Annunciation*.

Improvements have also been made in the framing and mounting of the pictures. The many fragments of altarpieces pose a particular problem. For these, special mounts have been made which allow them to be seen as incomplete pictures, without frames. Pictures with original frames, such as the van Eyck *Man in a Turban*, have been removed from the protective 'boxes' in which they were displayed, and, again with the aid of special metal fixings, are now exhibited without additional framing. In other cases framing work has been undertaken for scholarly or

BELOW
Restoring the frame of Crivelli's *Virgin and Child with Saint Jerome and Saint Sebastian* in the Gallery's frame workshop.

RIGHT
A conservator at work on the restoration of Jacopo di Cione's San Pier Maggiore altarpiece.

aesthetic reasons. Where original frames are lacking, pictures are shown as often as possible in good antique frames. A number have been refitted in Victorian pastiche frames, which until recently were considered inauthentic and were replaced by modern slips – often with unfortunate consequences. An example is the extraordinary *Demidoff Altarpiece* by Crivelli, which has a remarkable mid-nineteenth-century frame, the design of which is based on original frames of the second half of the fifteenth century found in the Marches and the Veneto. The panels of this altarpiece have now been returned to their frame, having been shown frameless for a number of years. The frame has had to be modified. The panels were originally arranged in the frame in three tiers, creating a monumental altarpiece. However, it was recently discovered that the four panels of the upper tier in fact came from a second altarpiece by Crivelli from the same church – San Domenico in Ascoli Piceno. The top tier has therefore been removed and a new crenellated top made for the frame. Two of the removed panels now hang either side of the *Demidoff Altarpiece* in what were parts of the original frame.

The *Demidoff Altarpiece*, 1476, by Carlo Crivelli, newly displayed in its ornate Victorian frame.

FROM THE TOP of the grand staircase a view extends westward across the three northernmost galleries of the new wing to Cima's large altarpiece, *The Incredulity of Saint Thomas*, which, with its life-size figures, perspectival recession and naturalistic light, gives an astonishing illusion of life, even at a great distance. But this is one of the latest works in the new galleries, painted in Venice during the last years of the fifteenth century and the first of the sixteenth, and will be encountered again at the end of our tour.

The first room, Room 51, comprises both the beginning and the end of the Early Renaissance collection, with paintings dating from the years around 1300 at the south end of the room, and the work of Leonardo and his followers, dating from the very beginning of the sixteenth century, at the north end. In Giotto's little panel of the *Pentecost* of about 1306–12 can be seen the beginnings of the Renaissance concern with naturalism and three-dimensionality; in Leonardo's *Virgin of the Rocks*, painted almost 200 years later in about 1508, the painted illusion of living beings in a natural setting has been perfected, and to it is added an unfathomable psychological depth which is new.

Turning left, into Room 52, we return to the beginnings of the collection. Most of the paintings in this room are fragments of Tuscan altarpieces painted during the first half of the fourteenth century. Among them are works by the great Sienese artist Duccio, including three jewel-like panels from his gigantic altarpiece, the *Maestà*, completed in 1311 for Siena Cathedral, and a small triptych of *The Virgin and Child with Saints*, exhibited in a case in the middle of the room. All are typified by glowing colours and a sinuous linear style which stem from Byzantine art. Similar in style are the fragments of an altarpiece painted in about 1325 for Santa Croce in Florence by Ugolino di Nerio, a follower of Duccio. On either side of the window are fourteenth-century sculptures of the Virgin and Child, on loan from the Victoria and Albert Museum, which would originally have been painted in colours similar to the paintings.

After the small works of Room 52, the great altarpieces in Room 53 come as a surprise, and give a truer idea of the scale and richness of church art in the fourteenth century. Most of these come from Florence and date from the second half of the century. Opposite the entrance are assembled the major parts of Jacopo di Cione's great altarpiece depicting *The Coronation of the Virgin*, painted for San Pier Maggiore in Florence in 1370–1. Like other altarpieces in this room it is highly ornate and richly embellished with gold and painted and stamped patterns. In a case in this room is one of the great treasures of the National Gallery, *The Wilton Diptych*, which shows King Richard II of England being presented to the Virgin and Child by three saints. The authorship is unknown, although it may be the work of a French court artist of about 1395. In the refinement of its style and the delicacy of its execution it is unmatched by any surviving painting of this period.

In the next room, Room 54, we find fifteenth-century paintings from Florence and Siena. Here is Lorenzo Monaco's charming altarpiece *The Coronation of the Virgin* of about 1414, which recalls the decorative style

The Annunciation, completed 1311, by Duccio.

of the previous century. In stark contrast is Masaccio's *Virgin and Child* of 1426, in which the figures have the massive solidity of sculpture and occupy a defined pictorial space. A similar response to three-dimensional form can be seen in the two pairs of saints possibly begun by Masaccio and completed by his associate, Masolino. Masaccio transformed the character of Italian art, but for a while a more conservative approach and a more decorative style continued to flourish in Siena, as can be seen in Sassetta's beautiful *Scenes from the Life of Saint Francis*, fragments from an altarpiece completed in 1444.

Room 55 is dominated by Uccello's *Battle of San Romano*, one of a series of three paintings commemorating this Florentine victory made in the 1450s for the Medici family. It is one of the earliest secular works in the Collection and shows the artist grappling with the problems of representing men and horses in movement. Also painted for the Medici, possibly to serve as bedheads, are Fra Filippo Lippi's *Seven Saints* and

The Wilton Diptych, c. 1395, French School (?).

LIBERTAS · ·ECCLESIASTICA·

ABOVE
Portrait of a Woman, 1420–30,
by Robert Campin.

OPPOSITE
The Annunciation, with Saint Emidius,
1486, by Carlo Crivelli.

Annunciation. Pisanello, who worked for the courts of Ferrara and Mantua, is represented here by two small devotional works, *The Vision of Saint Eustace* and *The Virgin and Child with Saints George and Anthony Abbot*.

The last of the eastern range of rooms, Room 56, a small unusually shaped room with oak skirtings, is devoted to four artists, Jan van Eyck, Robert Campin, Rogier van der Weyden and Petrus Christus, who worked in the southern Netherlands during the first half of the fifteenth century. They are therefore contemporary with the artists represented in Rooms 54 and 55, including Masaccio, Sassetta, Uccello and Fra Filippo Lippi, but the differences in their works are immediately apparent. The Northern paintings are all small in scale and naturalistic in detail. While nearly all Italian paintings of this date are in egg tempera, these are executed in oil-based paint, which gives them extraordinary depth and richness. Here, for the first time, we see portrait painting as we now know it, with precise observation and close rendering of features and expression. The Collection is remarkably rich in Netherlandish portraits of this period, and greatest of them all is the double portrait of Giovanni Arnolfini and Giovanna Cenami, '*The Arnolfini Marriage*' – a detailed and convincing depiction of a married couple in a room of the period, signed by the artist and dated 1434. Here too are portraits by Campin, van der Weyden and Petrus Christus, as well as others by van Eyck, each of which reveals a particular, individual human being. In this, above all, lies the great contribution of the North to the Renaissance.

Returning to Room 55 and taking the door to the left we enter the central range of rooms at the southern end. These four lofty rooms, which are linked by large arched openings lined with pietra serena, were designed to hold the majority of the Italian paintings of the second half of the fifteenth century, and in particular the group of great altarpieces of this period. The southernmost room, Room 57, contains altarpieces and smaller devotional works by Carlo Crivelli, Francesco del Cossa and Cosimo Tura, who worked respectively in the Marches, Bologna and Ferrara. On the south wall at the end of the main vista is Crivelli's *Demidoff Altarpiece* of 1476, a highly ornate polyptych painted for the high altar of San Domenico at Ascoli Piceno. The panels were assembled – with others now removed – for Prince Anatole Demidoff, who bought them in 1852; the elaborate frame, modelled on the kind of frame that many of Crivelli's paintings originally had, is also of that date. Another work by Crivelli in this room is *The Annunciation*, 1486, which shows the Angel Gabriel, accompanied by Saint Emidius holding a model of the town of Ascoli, kneeling outside a house within which we see the Virgin at prayer. The architectural perspective and intricate detail of this recently cleaned picture combine to make it one of the most remarkable in the Collection. Crivelli, Cossa and Tura were all influenced by the great Paduan painter Andrea Mantegna, whose early *Agony in the Garden* hangs in this room, close to a painting of the same subject, of 1465, by his Venetian brother-in-law, Giovanni Bellini. More examples of their work will be seen in Room 61.

The adjacent room to the north, Room 58, contains Florentine works of the same period by Botticelli and his followers, notably Filippino Lippi. They are characterised by a linear grace and clear bright colours. Although most are religious subjects (among them three treatments of *The Adoration of the Kings*, two by Botticelli and one by Filippino), they include one of the most celebrated secular paintings of the period, *Venus and Mars*, painted about 1485, which reflects a new sympathy for the nude and for pagan themes, while epitomising the attenuated elegance of Botticelli's figure style.

In Room 59 are represented other Florentine artists of the latter part of the century: Piero di Cosimo, Baldovinetti, Verrocchio, and Antonio and Piero del Pollaiuolo. The room is dominated by the huge *Martyrdom of Saint Sebastian* of 1475 by the Pollaiuolo brothers, in which the male figure is shown with anatomical accuracy in a number of dynamic poses. While this contrived but nonetheless naturalistic picture with its extensive landscape represents the scientific and analytical interests of Florentine artists, the altarpiece on the opposite wall of *The Assumption of the Virgin*, of 1474, by the Sienese artist Matteo di Giovanni shows with its gold ground and disjunctions of scale that at the same date a stylised and decorative approach continued to characterise painting in Siena. However, while these dominate by their scale, other pictures in this room surpass them in beauty: for example, Baldovinetti's exquisite *Portrait of a Lady in Yellow*, the entrancing *Tobias and the Angel* by a follower of Verrocchio, and Piero di Cosimo's sad and magical picture of a satyr mourning the death of a nymph.

The last room in this central sequence, Room 60, which includes paintings by Perugino and Raphael, we return to later. First we retrace our steps to Room 57 and turn right into the western range of rooms, which terminates on our left in Room 66. This is given to Piero della Francesca, one of the greatest and most fascinating painters of the fifteenth century. The Gallery is fortunate in having no less than three works by this outstanding artist: *The Baptism of Christ*, an early work with statuesque figures standing in an Umbrian landscape; *Saint Michael*, one of a number of figures of saints which made up an altarpiece; and *The Nativity*, a late, unfinished and partly damaged work, influenced in its design by Netherlandish painting of the type shown in Room 64. *The Baptism of Christ* hangs in a shallow niche on the south wall, at the end of a vista from Room 63.

Rooms 65 and 64 are linked by a wide opening and are intended to be viewed as a pair of complementary spaces. Paintings by Italian and Netherlandish artists working in the middle years of the fifteenth century are here juxtaposed, to emphasise the high regard in which Netherlandish art was held throughout Europe at that time. Among the Italian works are the Gallery's superb collection of paintings by Antonello da Messina, a Sicilian whose art was strongly affected by Netherlandish painting. His *Saint Jerome in his Study* of around 1475–6 with its detailed interior and glimpses of views through windows has a distinctly Northern feel, while his *Portrait of a Man*, also of about 1475,

ABOVE
Tobias and the Angel, c. 1470–5, by a follower of Andrea del Verrocchio.

BELOW
Portrait of a Man, c. 1475, by Antonello da Messina.

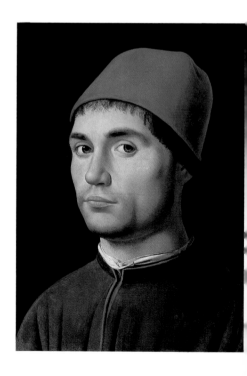

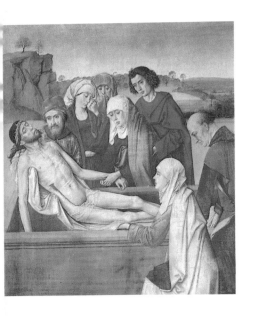

has all the intensity of characterisation we associate with Netherlandish portraiture. Similarly small in scale is *The Blood of the Redeemer*, an early work by Giovanni Bellini, whose work Antonello knew well.

Alongside these and other Italian paintings hang works by two Netherlandish artists: Hans Memlinc and Dieric Bouts. *The Entombment* by Bouts, a rare surviving example of a Netherlandish painting on linen, dating from about 1450–60, came from an Italian source and may even have been painted for an Italian patron. Memlinc's *Donne Triptych* of around 1475 was almost certainly commissioned by an Englishman. The triptych, which is displayed in a case, shows Sir John Donne and his family with the Virgin and saints. Although it is not in its original frame it is one of the few examples of Northern altarpieces in the National Gallery to have survived complete, and with its painted backs. Two panels of saints from another altarpiece by Memlinc are also displayed so that their backs, which show a landscape with cranes, can be seen.

The next room, Room 63, contains German paintings from the fifteenth century. The earliest is *The Trinity with Christ Crucified* of around 1410, by an unknown artist, which occupies the centre of the west wall. From this point can be seen – across the width of the building – the roughly contemporaneous *Wilton Diptych* in Room 53. While the latter is a small, delicate, portable work, the Austrian *Trinity* is a large altarpiece (now without its shutters), powerfully hieratic in conception, and dominated by a massive architectural throne. The Gallery has a particularly strong holding of works from northwest Germany, by artists working in Cologne and Westphalia. They include a shutter of an altarpiece by Stephan Lochner, showing three saints, painted in a sweetly expressive style, an exquisite panel of *The Presentation in the Temple* by the Master of the Life of the Virgin, and three powerful works by the Master of the Saint Bartholomew Altarpiece, among them the large panel of *Saints Peter and Dorothy*, which exemplifies the expressive and decorative quality of German painting in the fifteenth century. Also in this room are three striking portraits from southern Germany: the *Portrait of a Woman of the Hofer Family* of about 1470, Dürer's portrait of his father of 1497, and the recently purchased *Portrait of Alexander Mornauer* of about the 1470s by the Master of the Mornauer Portrait.

The next room in this sequence, Room 62, includes later Netherlandish paintings by Gerard David, Quinten Massys and Hieronymus Bosch, a part of a painting by the French Master of Moulins and two fragments of altarpiece shutters, painted on both sides, by Simon Marmion, a Netherlandish painter active in France. In *Christ Mocked*, of around 1490–1500, Bosch presents us with a vivid representation of Christ's tormentors. Very different is David's altarpiece *The Virgin and Child with Saints and Donor*, of about 1500–11, with its air of serene calm and a beautiful setting of a walled garden.

In Room 61, the largest room of the western galleries, we return to Italy – to Venice at the end of the fifteenth century. The room is dominated by Cima's large altarpiece of *The Incredulity of Saint Thomas* of 1504, which we first saw at a distance on our entry into the new galleries, but it also contains superb works by Andrea Mantegna and Giovanni Bellini. Here are Bellini's *Doge Leonardo Loredan* of about 1501–5, one of the finest achievements of portraiture of the period, and his *Madonna of the Meadow* of around 1500–5, with its serene landscape background, which, while quintessentially Italian, owes much to Netherlandish realism. Among the paintings by Mantegna are four which imitate carved stone reliefs, demonstrating his passionate interest in antique art.

We now return to Room 60, the northernmost of the central galleries, from which a view extends southward through the series of broad arched doorways to Crivelli's *Demidoff Altarpiece* in Room 57, surely one of the most impressive vistas in any gallery. At the northern end of this enfilade is *The Crucified Christ*, an early work by Raphael of about 1503, which shows the influence of the Umbrian painter Perugino. Here too is a slightly later altarpiece by Raphael, *The Ansidei Madonna*, as well as other large altarpieces of around 1500 by Filippino Lippi and Lorenzo Costa. Perugino is represented by three panels from one of his finest altarpieces, showing the Virgin and Child with saints in a landscape.

We end where we began, in Room 51, with Leonardo da Vinci. In a small room entered from two doors on either side of *The Virgin of the Rocks* is Leonardo's famous Cartoon of *The Virgin and Child with Saint John the Baptist and Saint Anne* of about 1507–8. This is a rare example of a large preparatory drawing, and as works on paper are especially sensitive it is exhibited in a special case in reduced light. It has long been admired and, even more than *The Virgin of the Rocks*, reveals Leonardo's softness of modelling, psychological complexity, and sophistication of composition. It is a fitting preparation for the great masterpieces of the sixteenth century which are shown across the bridge of the Sainsbury Wing in the galleries of the old building.

ABOVE
The Painter's Father, 1497,
by Albrecht Dürer.

OPPOSITE
The Doge Leonardo Loredan,
c. 1501–5, by Giovanni Bellini.

BELOW
Cartoon: The Virgin and Child with Saint John the Baptist and Saint Anne,
c. 1507–8, by Leonardo da Vinci.

IOANNES BELLINVS

Floor Plans

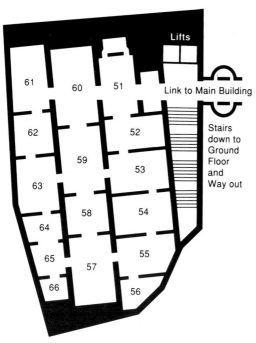

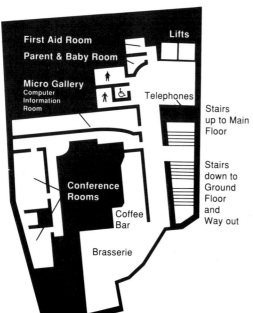

MAIN FLOOR

Early Renaissance Galleries

The Main Floor Collection is divided into four parts, located in four different areas of the National Gallery building:

Sainsbury Wing: Painting from 1260 to 1510
West Wing: Painting from 1510 to 1600
North Wing: Painting from 1600 to 1700
East Wing: Painting from 1700 to 1920

The paintings in the Sainsbury Wing are arranged as follows:

51 Italian: Giotto, Leonardo da Vinci
52 Italian before 1400
53 Italian before 1400; The Wilton Diptych
54 Italian: Masaccio, Sassetta
55 Italian: Uccello
56 Netherlandish: van Eyck
57 Italian: Crivelli, Tura
58 Italian: Botticelli
59 Italian: Pollaiuolo, Piero di Cosimo
60 Italian: Raphael
61 Italian: Bellini, Mantegna
62 Netherlandish and French: David, Massys
63 German
64 Netherlandish and Italian
65 Italian: Antonello, Bellini
66 Italian: Piero della Francesca

FIRST FLOOR

Micro Gallery: Computer Information Room (sponsored by the American Express Foundation). Using interactive screens, detailed information on individual artists and paintings from the National Gallery Collection can be summoned at a touch and, if required, printed out.

Brasserie and Coffee Bar Paintings in the Brasserie (donated by English Estates) are by Paula Rego, Associate Artist at the National Gallery during 1990. A Café is also situated in the Main Building.

Conference Rooms Equipped with audio-visual facilities, these rooms are designed for use by special groups for talks, seminars and receptions.

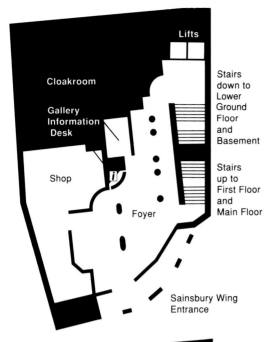

GROUND FLOOR

Sainsbury Wing Information Desk Information on daily events is shown on a large screen beside the Desk, nearby are large floor plans and general Gallery information for visitors.

The National Gallery Shop Books, exhibition catalogues, posters and postcards are available here. A second shop is located in the Main Building.

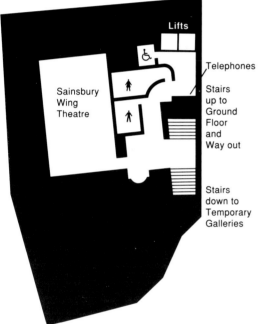

LOWER GROUND FLOOR

Sainsbury Wing Theatre Lunchtime slide lectures and films are held here throughout the year. The theatre seats 340 people and contains an induction loop for the hard of hearing as well as spaces for wheel-chairs. It also accommodates conferences and small-scale musical and dramatic performances.

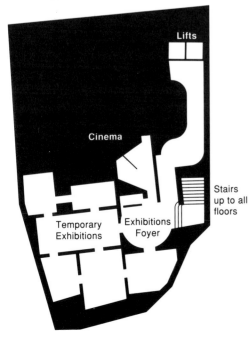

BASEMENT

Temporary Exhibition Galleries There are six rooms of varying size to accommodate a range of special exhibitions. Loan exhibitions are shown here on a regular basis.

Cinema Video and tape/slide programmes are shown here to accompany exhibitions. It accommodates approximately 50 people seated, with additional standing space.

Gallery Information

Admission free

Open

Monday to Saturday, 10.00 am–6.00 pm
Sunday, 2.00–6.00 pm

Closed

24, 25 and 26 December, 1 January, Good Friday and May Day

The National Gallery Shops and Information Desks

Open: Monday to Saturday, 10.00 am–5.40 pm
Sunday, 2–5.40 pm

Micro Gallery: Computer Information Room

Open: Monday to Saturday, 10.00 am–5.30 pm
Sunday, 2–5.30 pm

Brasserie, Coffee Bar and Café

Open: Monday to Saturday, 10.00 am–5 pm
Sunday, 2–5 pm

Lectures, Films and Guided Tours

Lunchtime slide lectures and films are held in the Sainsbury Wing Theatre throughout the year. Details of these, guided tours and other special events held in the Gallery can be obtained from the Information Desks, and are listed in the current issue of *National Gallery News*.

Illustration Acknowledgements

LONDON
British Library: page 9.
Dulwich Picture Gallery: page 26 (bottom right), by permission of the Governors of Dulwich Picture Gallery.
Times Newspapers Limited: pages 8 and 35.
PHILADELPHIA
Venturi, Scott Brown and Associates, Inc.:
pages 12 (top left) photo. John T. Miller and 13 (top left, photo: Tom Bernard).

Photographers

Astrid Athen: pages 11, 14 and 17 (bottom left).
Colin Harvey: pages 10, 23 (left) and 33.
Phil Starling: front cover, pages 6, 15–22, 25–7, 34 and 37.